DISCARD

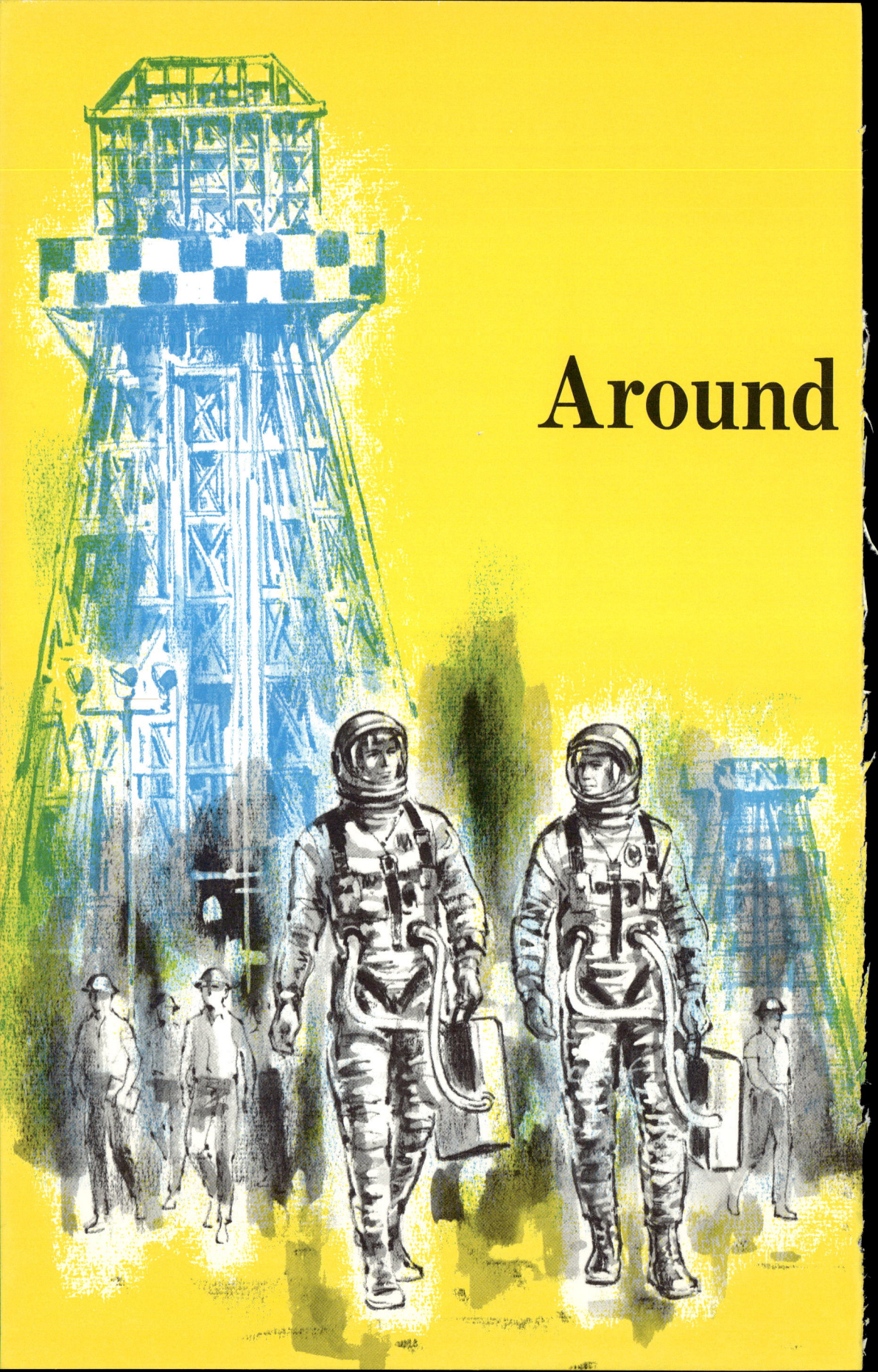

by Rocco V. Feravolo

the World in Ninety Minutes
The Journey of Two Astronauts

illustrated by William Steinel

Lothrop, Lee & Shepard Co., Inc. NEW YORK

The author wishes to express his gratitude to Mr. Ralph Gibson and Mr. William O'Donald of the Public Affairs Office, NASA, for reading and criticizing the manuscript.

Text copyright © 1968 by Rocco V. Feravolo / Illustrations copyright © 1968 by William Steinel
Library of Congress Catalog Card Number: 68-27708. Printed in the United States of America. All rights reserved.
1 2 3 4 5 72 71 70 69 68

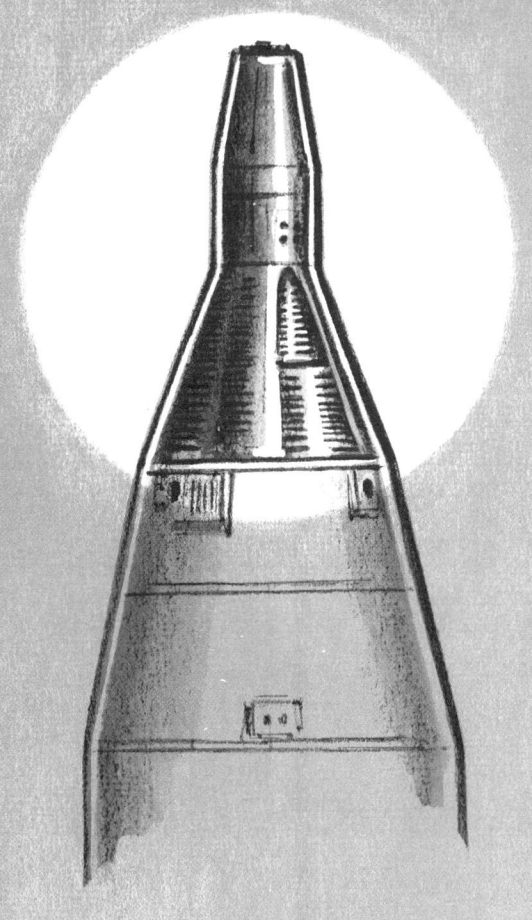

These two astronauts are about to go for a ride in space. Their rocket towers eleven stories above the launching pad in a frame called a gantry. An elevator in the gantry carries them to a tiny spacecraft on top of the rocket.

In the spacecraft the men are strapped to couches, which will support them as the rocket speeds skyward.

All around are instruments, which will tell them such things as the temperature, the amount of oxygen they have for breathing, and the air pressure—the force with which the air in the spacecraft presses on the astronauts' bodies.

All this time the countdown has been going on in a control room about a mile away. When the countdown reaches zero, the rocket will roar into space and take the astronauts with it.

Now the final count begins. Eight, seven, six, five, four, three, two, one—zero! The rocket is lifting off the pad!

This is a multistage rocket, built in sections, or stages. The bottom part is the first stage. It has to build up enough thrust to lift not only itself but also the second stage and the spacecraft off the ground and take them high

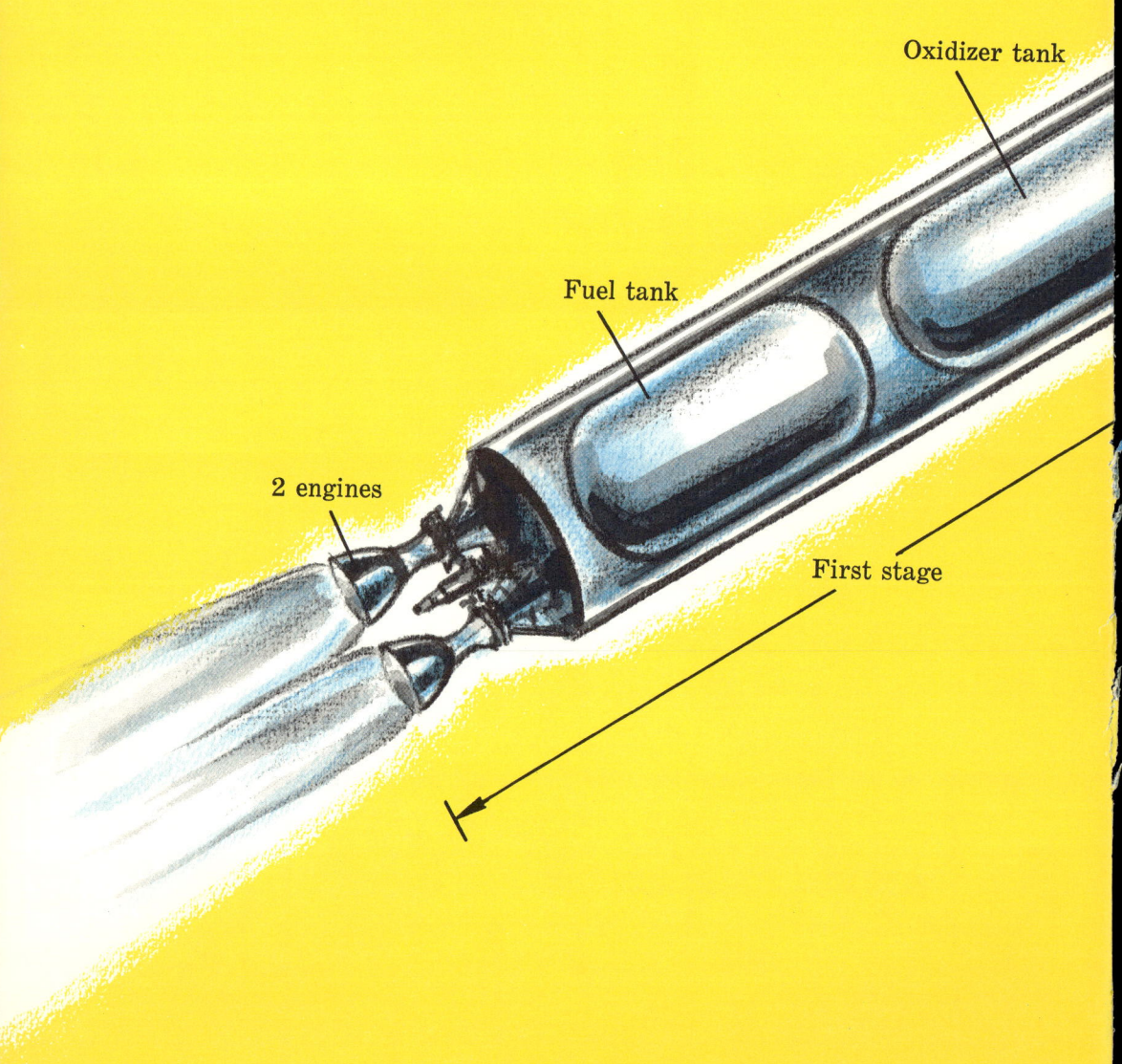

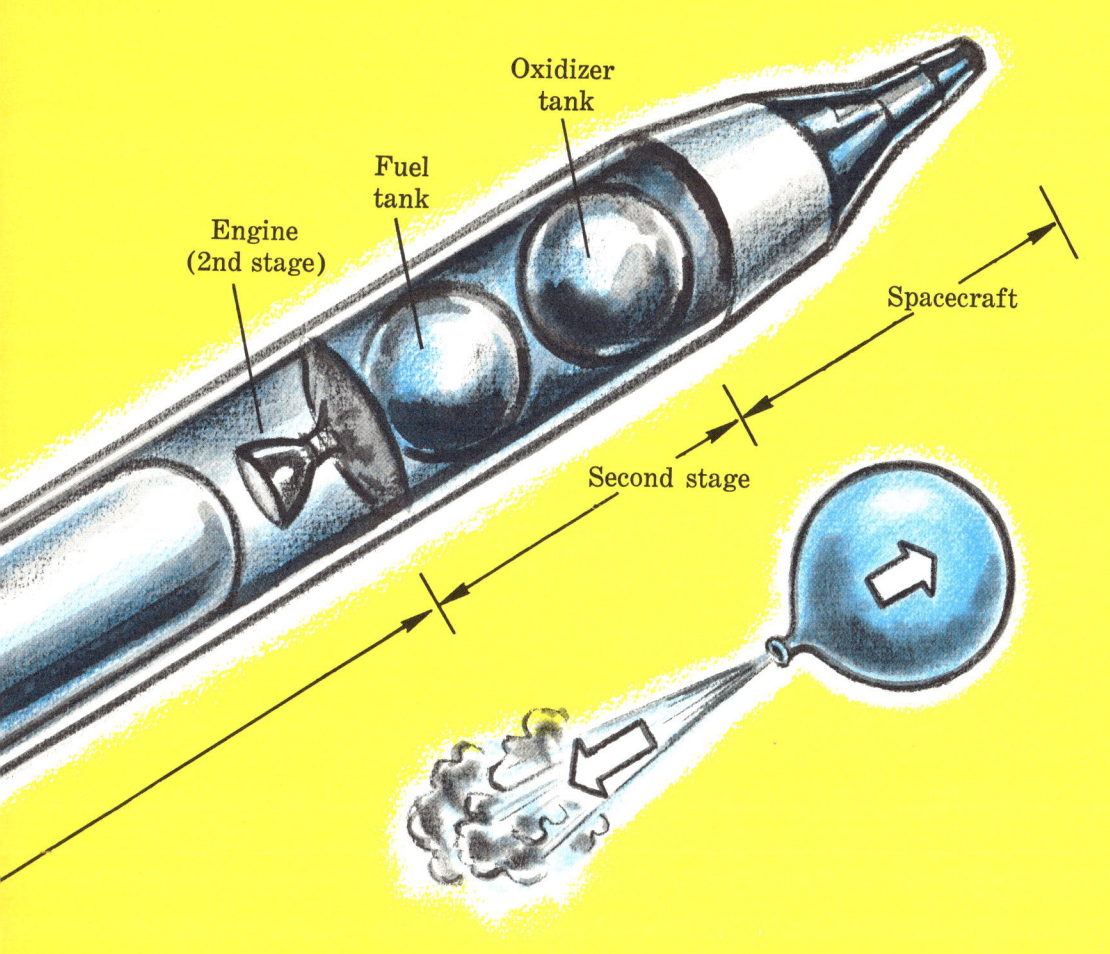

into the sky. It therefore has the largest engine and carries the most fuel. In its first minute off the pad a rocket uses as much fuel as a jet liner crossing the United States from California to New York.

Hot gases, roaring backward from the rocket's exhaust nozzle, kick forward on the rocket and propel it upward. As the speed builds up, the astronauts feel heavier and heavier. The weight of their bodies presses them hard against the couches. Their arms and legs are like lead. Soon they feel a force equal to eight times normal gravity.

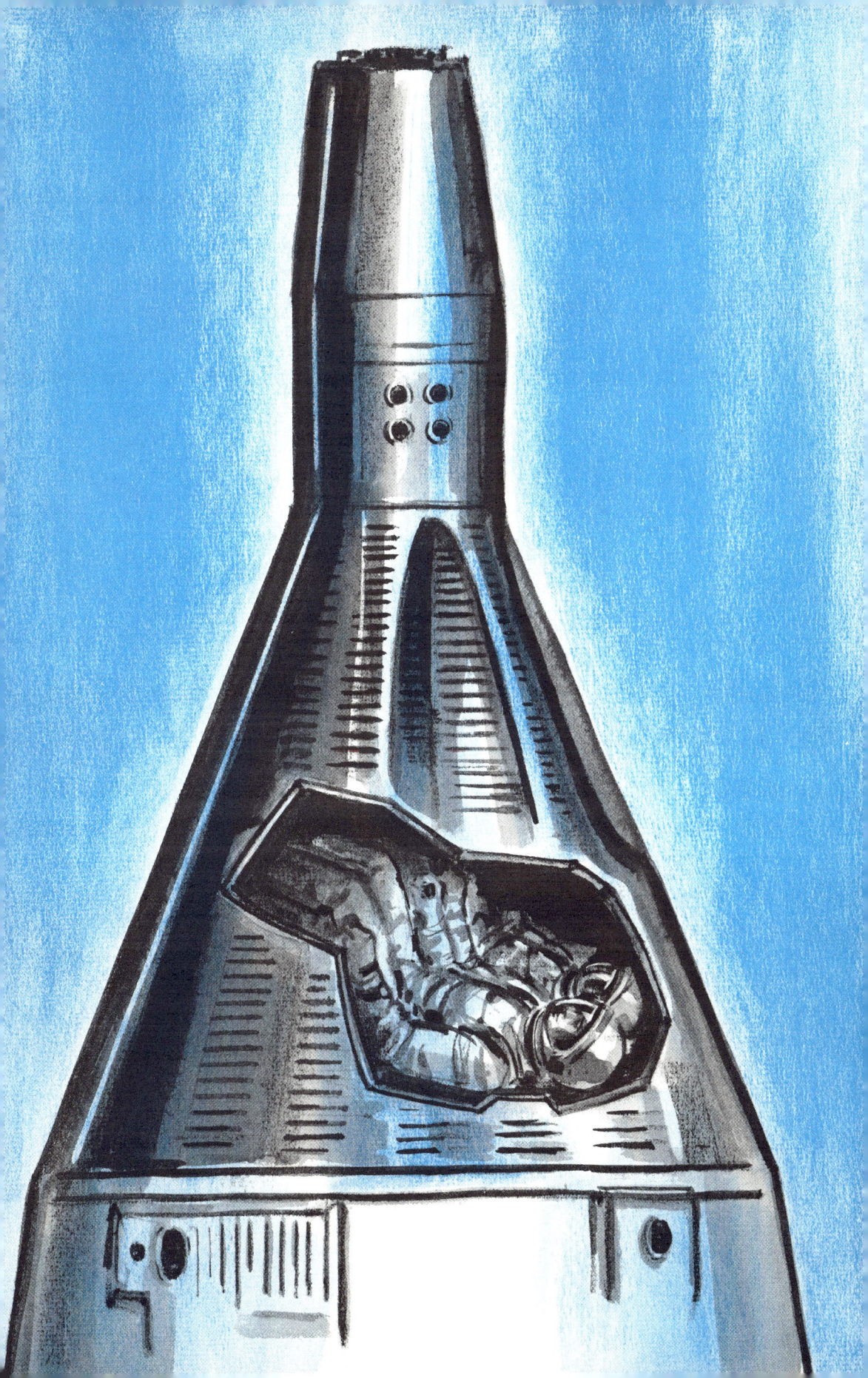

Gravity is the force that pulls things toward the center of the earth. If gravity did not exist, everything would float away.

On earth, gravity pulls on the body with a force of one "G," but the steadily increasing speed, or acceleration, of a rocket builds up this force to about eight G's. This is the same as eight times a person's usual weight, because weight is a measure of gravity. If one of the astronauts weighs 156 pounds, his weight at eight G's will be eight times 156, or 1248 pounds—more than half a ton.

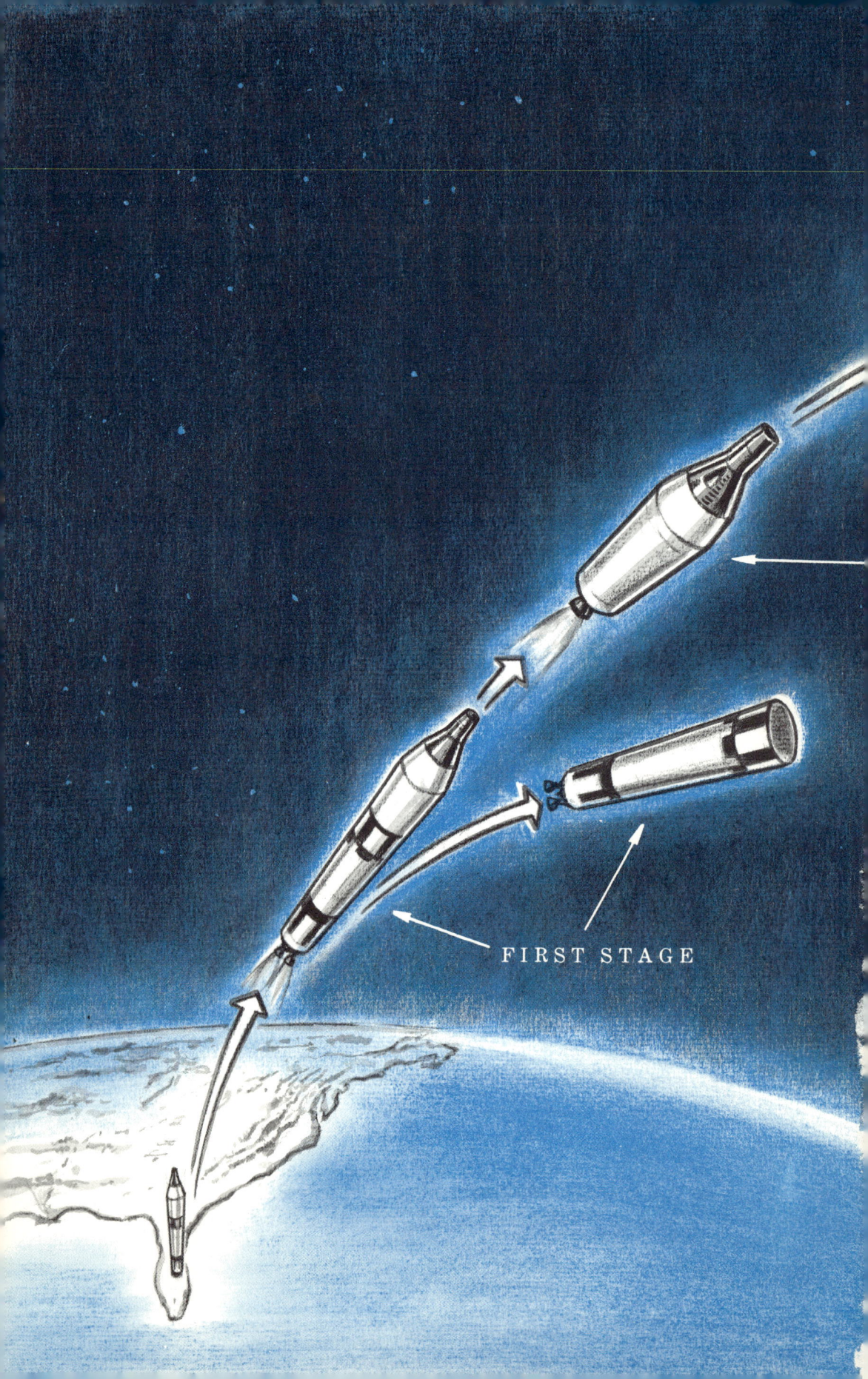

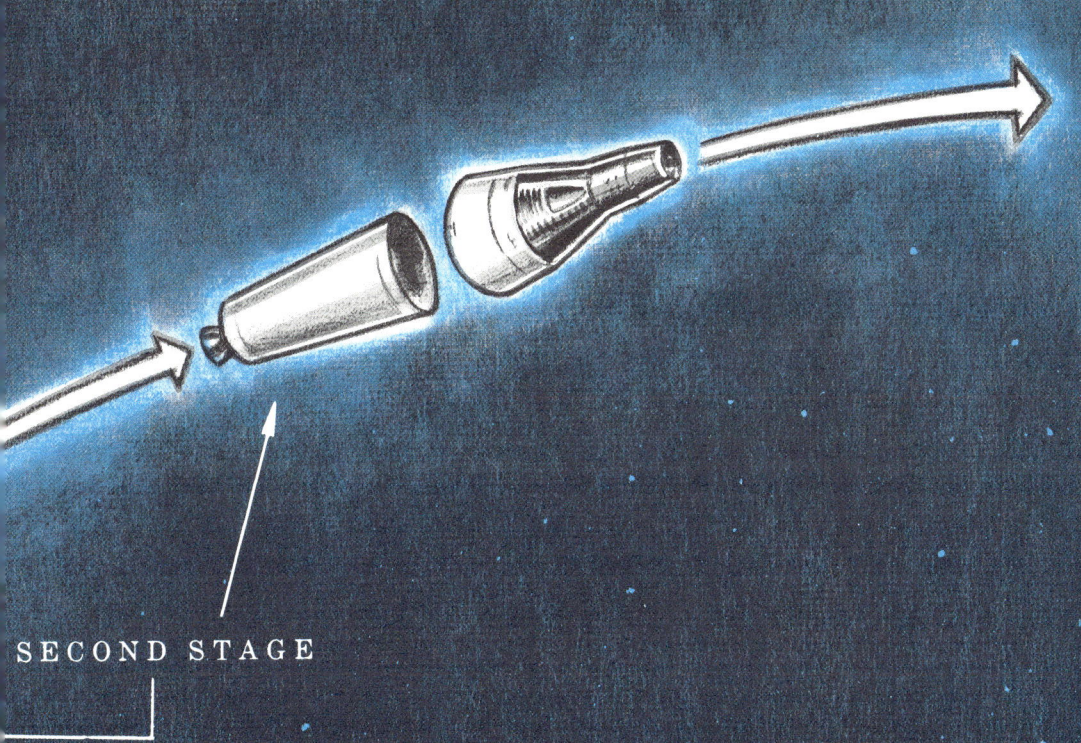

SECOND STAGE

As the first stage carries the rocket to a height of over forty miles, the G force begins to go down. The rocket is going about 6710 miles an hour when the fuel runs out, and the first stage automatically falls into the ocean.

Then the second stage fires and the astronauts are again flattened against their couches. This stage has a smaller engine and uses less fuel, because it has less weight to move and is now traveling through thinner air.

By the time the second stage falls away, the payload—another name for the spacecraft—is circling the earth without a motor at about 17,500 miles an hour—as fast as traveling across our entire country in ten minutes. In the blink of an eye, a spacecraft, traveling at 17,500 miles an hour, goes about five miles—or many times faster than a bullet.

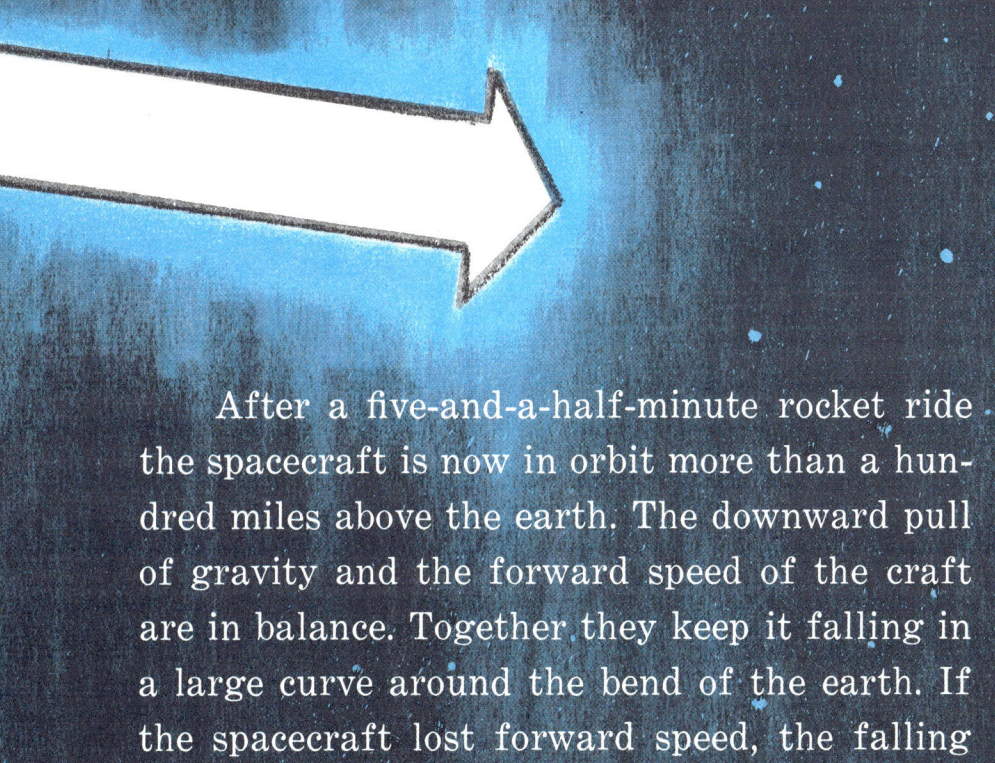

After a five-and-a-half-minute rocket ride the spacecraft is now in orbit more than a hundred miles above the earth. The downward pull of gravity and the forward speed of the craft are in balance. Together they keep it falling in a large curve around the bend of the earth. If the spacecraft lost forward speed, the falling speed would win out and the spacecraft would be pulled back to the ground.

When the astronauts are in orbit they are actually falling at a constant rate toward the earth in response to the pull of gravity. On earth they would feel this pull as their "weight," because the earth is between them and the pull of gravity. In space, however, men, objects, and spacecraft are all falling together. They feel no

weight, merely because there is nothing in the way to resist the fall.

If the astronauts were not strapped down they would float around the small cabin. A pen that gets loose does float around the spacecraft, bouncing off everything it touches. It does not fall to the floor because the floor is falling too.

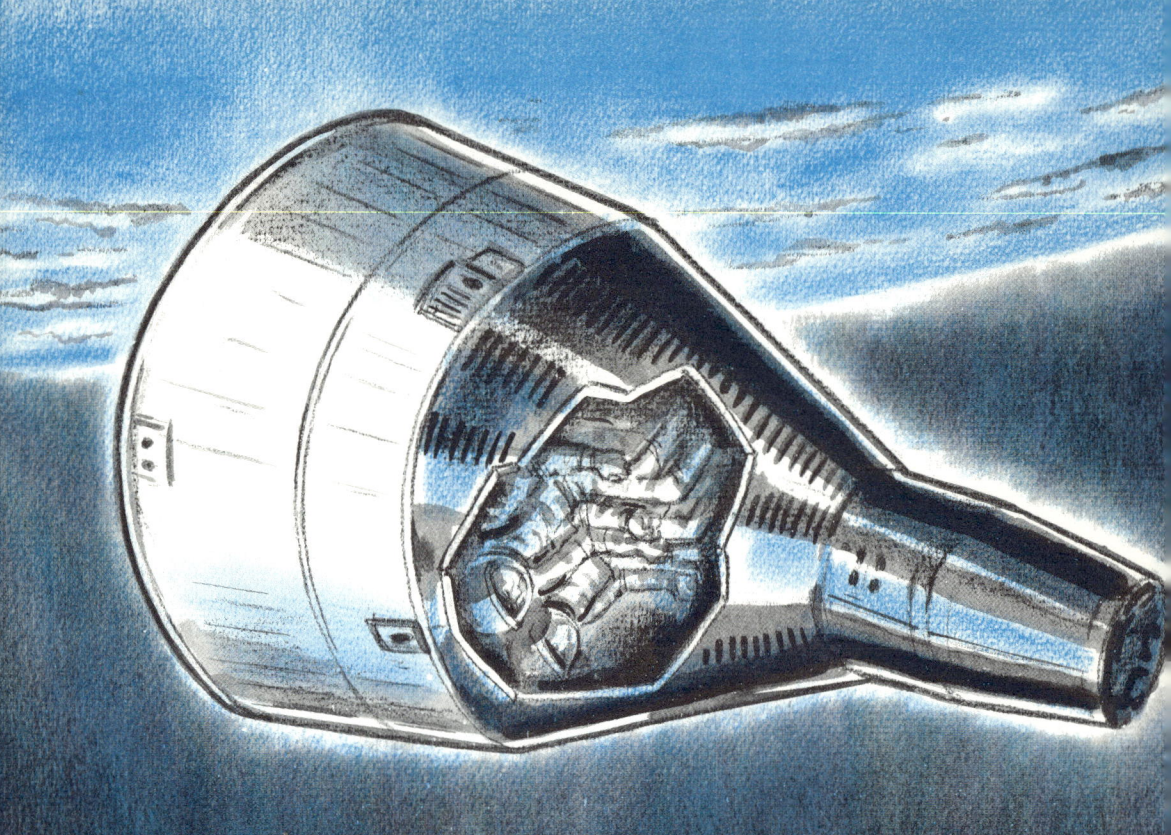

The spacecraft orbits the earth in only ninety minutes. As it travels, the astronauts may at times seem to be upside down. But they do not feel as if they are.

If you were to stand on your head on earth, you would feel gravity pulling the blood to it, and you would soon be uncomfortable. However, when you are upside down in a weightless state in space, the blood is not pulled to your head, because in this case your head is falling as fast as the blood is being pulled to it. As a result, the blood can never catch up!

After three ninety-minute orbits the astronauts gradually let the oxygen out of the cabin and put more oxygen in their space suits. When the cabin, like space, has no air in it, one of them opens the hatch and climbs outside. He is going to take a walk in space more than a hundred miles above the earth.

His space suit, made in twenty-one layers with a nylon cover, protects him from the extremely hot and cold temperatures and the bits of matter in space.

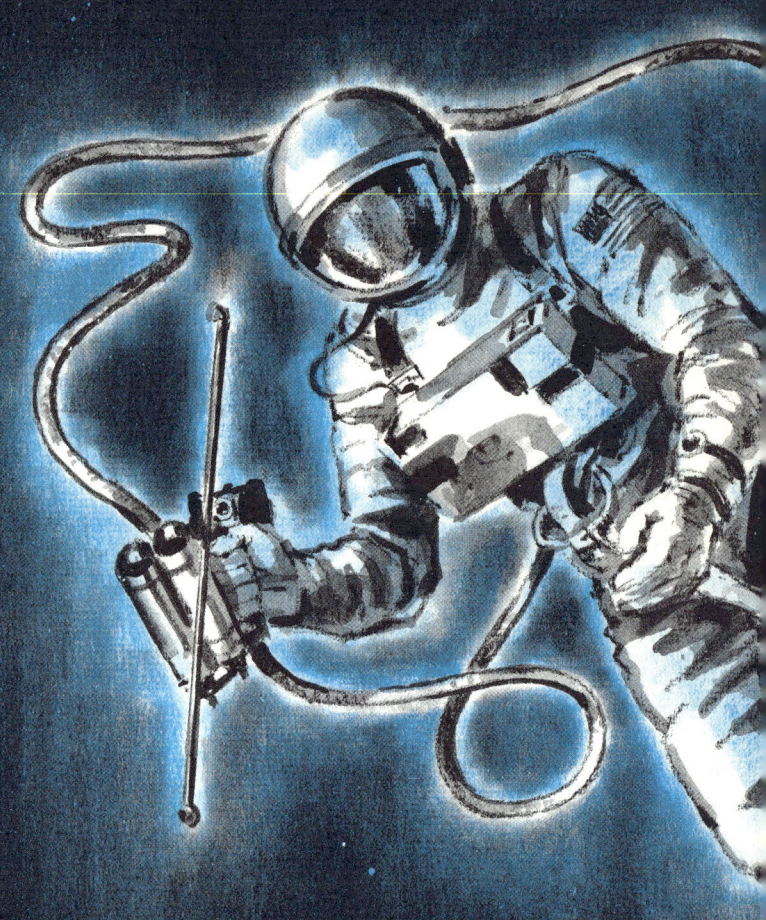

Connected to the space suit is the hose to the ship's oxygen supply. In case it doesn't work, the pack he carries will give the astronaut ten minutes of emergency oxygen. He also makes sure his Dacron lifeline is hooked to the spacecraft. If he drifted away, he would become an artificial satellite and circle the earth in a weightless condition for a long time at 17,500 miles an hour.

The astronaut's helmet has two strong visors. Special padded gloves allow him to touch either the hot sunny side of the spacecraft or its freezing dark side. In his hand he carries a jet gun powered by small tanks of compressed oxygen and provided with three nozzles. Pressure from the gun propels and turns him in space. By firing blasts from it he can go in any direction.

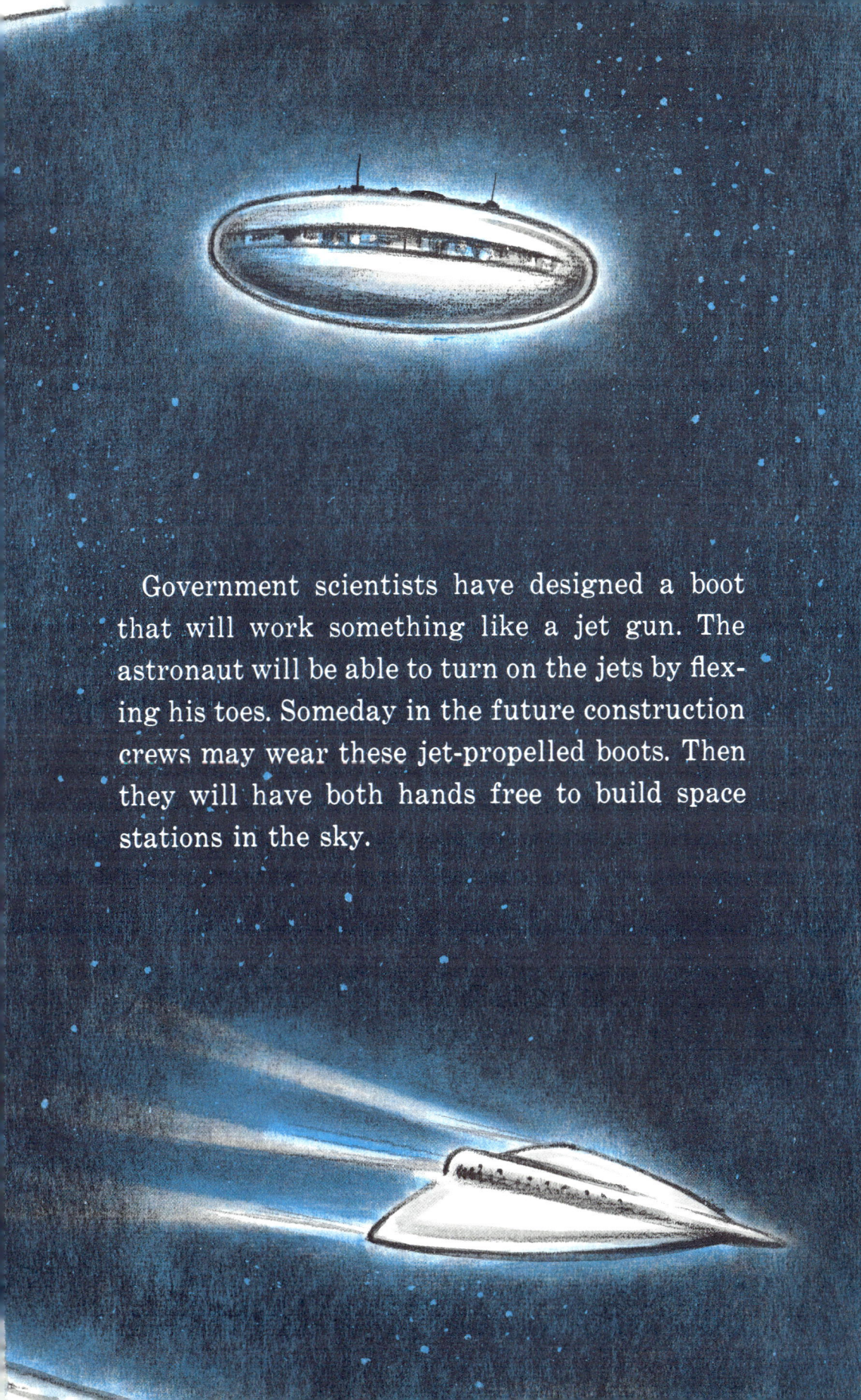

Government scientists have designed a boot that will work something like a jet gun. The astronaut will be able to turn on the jets by flexing his toes. Someday in the future construction crews may wear these jet-propelled boots. Then they will have both hands free to build space stations in the sky.

The space walker is surprised to notice that roads on the earth are visible in clear detail. From more than a hundred miles up he has a spectacular view.

But he must go back inside. He climbs through the open hatch and seals it shut. Then the astronauts refill the cabin with oxygen to the proper pressure.

Spacecraft — Retro-rocket section — Equipment section

The astronauts spend the time eating, sleeping, taking pictures, and performing other tasks. After four days they fire small rocket engines, called retro-rockets, to slow the spacecraft. The retro-rockets fire in the direction they are traveling and push them backward.

Spacecraft

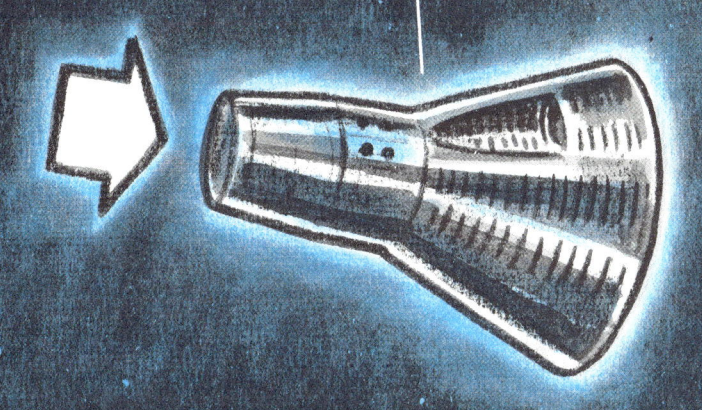

Retro-rocket section

Meanwhile, their position is being closely tracked in a control center below.

After the retro-rockets are discarded, the astronauts use other small rockets to point the curved heat shield on the blunt end of the spacecraft toward the earth.

When they are about fifty miles above the earth on their re-entry flight, they can feel the G's building up once more. Their ship has begun to plunge into the atmosphere, or cover of air around the earth.

The air rubs against the front of the spacecraft and makes it hot, just as rubbing the hands together makes them warm. However, the heat shield's outer surface is made of a material that starts to boil away instead of getting hotter.

The boiled-off particles from the shield carry away heat that might otherwise burn up the spacecraft.

The spacecraft is going to land in the ocean. At about 21,000 feet, a small parachute opens. This six-foot chute, called a drogue chute, steadies and slows the spacecraft as it falls. At 10,000 feet, at a speed of about 250 miles an hour, another larger chute opens. Sixty-three feet wide, this chute slows the spacecraft to a point where it will finally drop gently into the water.

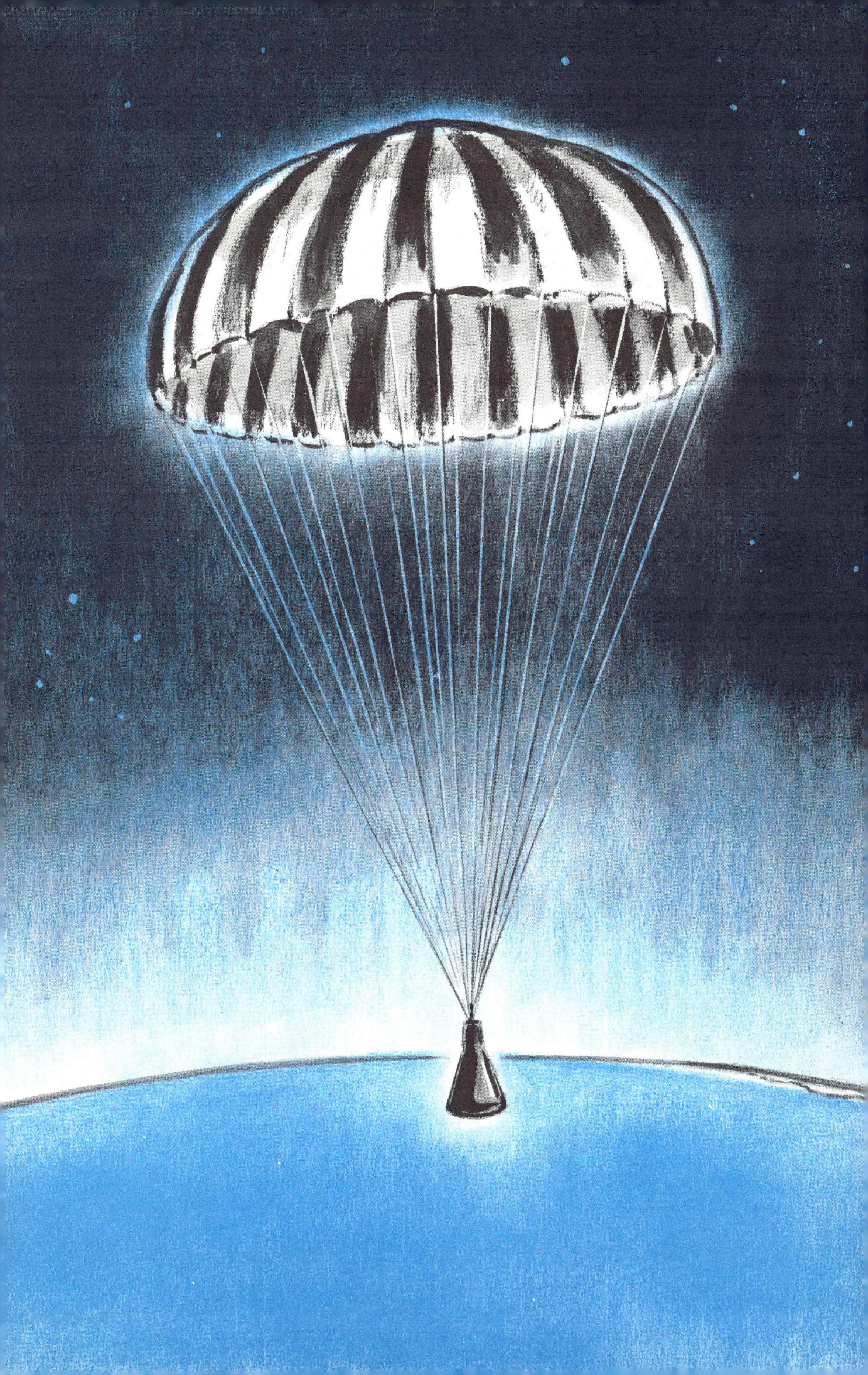

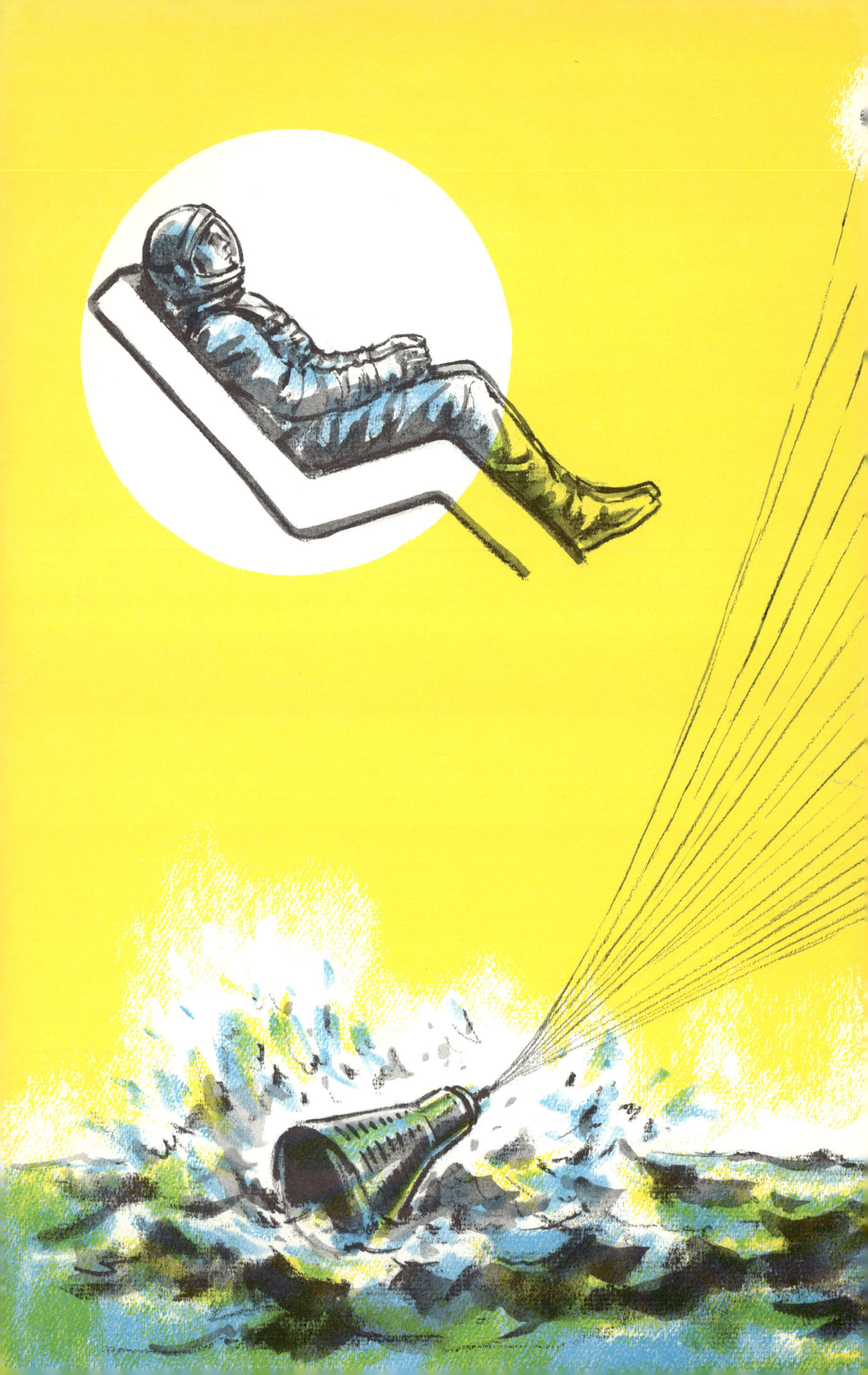

When the spacecraft hits the water, the couches cushion the impact for the astronauts.

They open the hatches. Soon several helicopters fly over, and Navy frogmen, or divers, alight from them. One of the helicopter pilots lowers a sling to the astronauts while the frogmen are hooking a line to the spacecraft. Finally both spacecraft and astronauts are flown to an aircraft carrier and landed on its deck.

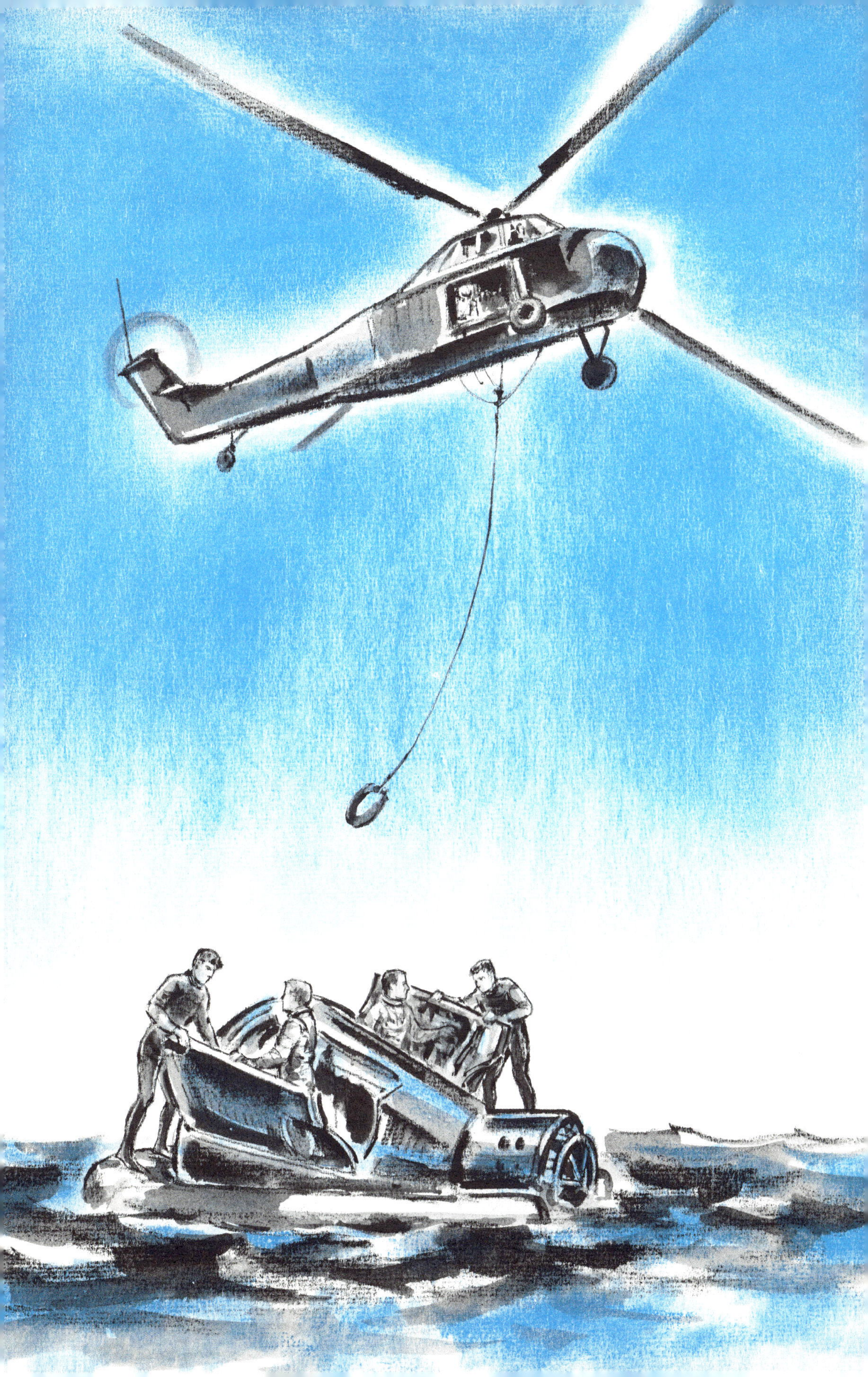

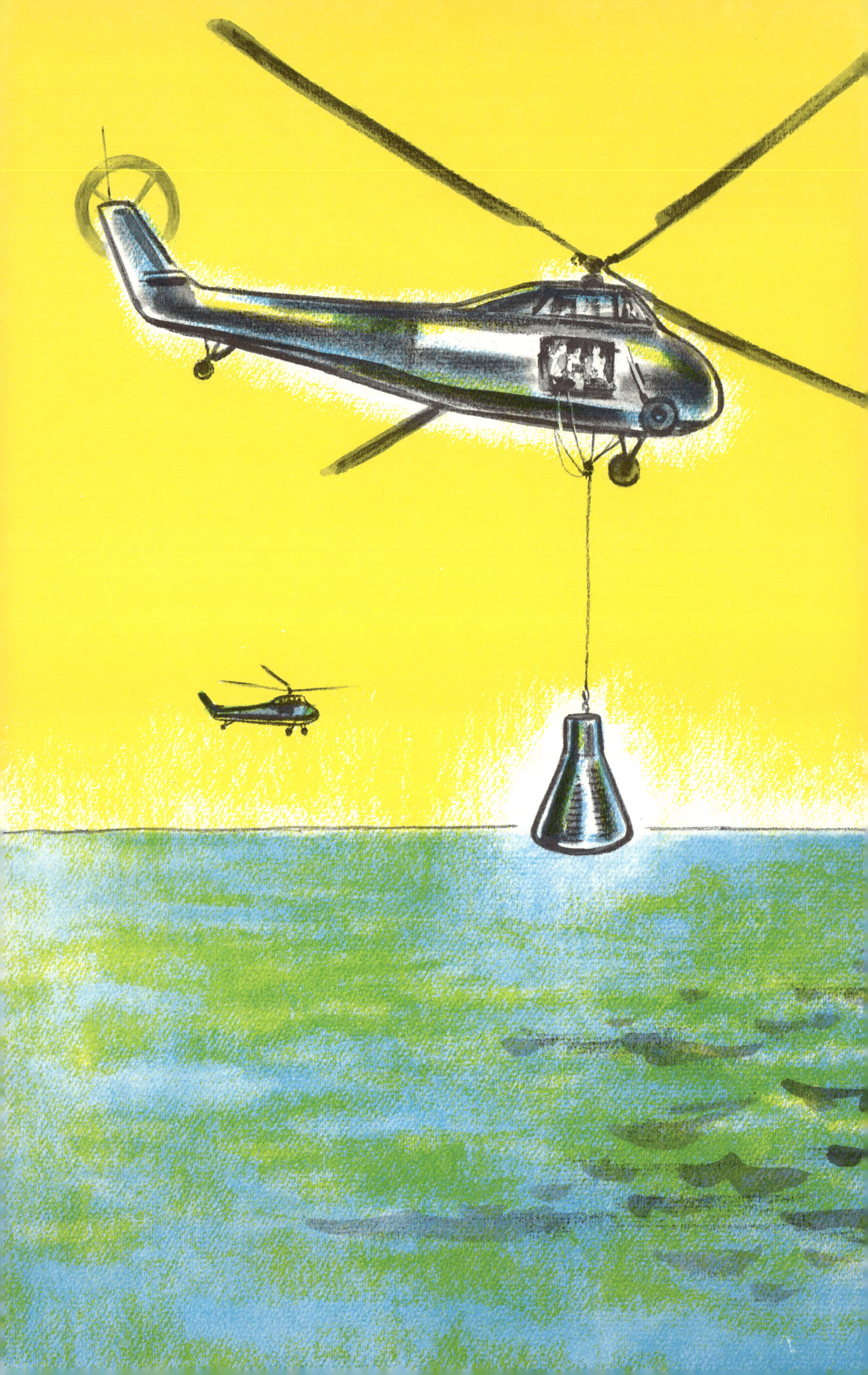

As the astronauts step out of the helicopter they are greeted by a cheering crowd of sailors.

Once again man has ventured into space and orbited the earth, adding to his knowledge of himself and his universe.

SPACE WORDS

AIR PRESSURE: the force with which air pushes on things.
ATMOSPHERE: the blanket of air around the earth.
COUNTDOWN: a backward count during which preparations are made for a space flight.
DROGUE CHUTE: a small parachute used to slow a landing spacecraft.
G: a unit showing the pull of gravity on a body.
GANTRY: a frame with platforms at different levels used to erect and service rockets before launching.
GRAVITY: the pull of the earth, or any celestial body, upon objects on or near it.
JET: a stream of liquid, gas, or vapor, forced through a nozzle.
JET-PROPELLED: the state of being pushed forward by the strong backward rush of jets.
LAUNCHING PAD: a fireproof platform used for sending off rockets or missiles.
ORBIT: to circle around; also, the path taken by one object revolving around another.
OXYGEN: a colorless, odorless, tasteless gas found in the earth's atmosphere, and necessary to all life on earth.
PAYLOAD: the cargo carried by and placed in space by a rocket.
RETRO-ROCKETS: extra rockets carried by a spacecraft, which are fired in the same direction to slow it down.
SATELLITE: a moon or other celestial body in orbit around a larger body; an ARTIFICIAL SATELLITE is made by man and placed in orbit by man.
SPACE: the region beyond the atmosphere of the earth.
SPACE STATION: a manned artificial satellite that will be used for scientific work or as a base for further space exploration.
WEIGHTLESS: seemingly unaffected by gravity.

Around the World in Ninety Minutes
The Journey of Two Astronauts
ROCCO V. FERAVOLO
illustrated by
WILLIAM STEINEL

In the blink of an eye a spacecraft orbiting the earth at about 17,500 miles an hour travels five miles. In ninety minutes it can go all the way around the world.

An explanation of what keeps this spacecraft in orbit is only part of the easily assimilated but valuable information furnished in this simply written story for the youngest readers of a Gemini space flight. The bold illustrations, an essential part of the book, ably assist Mr. Feravolo in interpreting such phenomena as gravity, weightlessness, and G's, and add reality to an exciting space walk more than a hundred miles above the earth.

This is a colorful introduction to space travel, which takes the reader along on the adventure from the moment the astronauts blast off from the launching pad to their final splashdown in the ocean.